T0113759

Landscapes of the Heart

Landscapes of the Heart

MARY R. CALLAHAN

authorHOUSE®

AuthorHouse™
1663 Liberty Drive
Bloomington, IN 47403
www.authorhouse.com
Phone: 1 (800) 839-8640

© 2015 Mary R. Callahan. All rights reserved.

No part of this book may be reproduced, stored in a retrieval system, or transmitted by any means without the written permission of the author.

Published by AuthorHouse 06/29/2015

ISBN: 978-1-5049-1983-8 (sc)
ISBN: 978-1-5049-1982-1 (e)

Print information available on the last page.

Any people depicted in stock imagery provided by Thinkstock are models, and such images are being used for illustrative purposes only. Certain stock imagery © Thinkstock.

This book is printed on acid-free paper.

Because of the dynamic nature of the Internet, any web addresses or links contained in this book may have changed since publication and may no longer be valid. The views expressed in this work are solely those of the author and do not necessarily reflect the views of the publisher, and the publisher hereby disclaims any responsibility for them.

Dedication

This book of poems is dedicated to my family, who fill me with great joy, and to my students at Bucks County Community College. As the beneficiary of a Cultural Incentive Grant, I am pleased to be able to present a poetry workshop to interested students during the Fall, 2015 semester using the works of masters (including my personal hero, Chris Bursk) and the grant-funded publication of fifty-five of my poems. It is my pleasure to contribute proceeds from sales of the book to the Bucks County Community College Student Scholarship Fund. It is my hope that this scholarship will be presented to a student with disabilities or a student majoring in English who desires to develop stronger creative writing skills.

I am honored by this award and grateful to Bucks County Community College for the opportunity to inspire future writers.

Mary R. Callahan, Ed.D.

Contents

Alzheimer's Lament

Bits and pieces of me seem
to float about aimlessly,
no safe harbor in sight.
My consciousness is scattered,
shattered like shards of glass
making blinding prisms in the sunlight.
Who are these people casting ephemeral glances
with futile hopes of my return?
They gently slip into the quicksand of my mind,
fleeting recollections of once-cherished connections,
leaving me with broken dreams.
Memories of my early days cloud recognition of today
as if I am being recreated anew.
Then darkness consumes me like black flame,
burning holes in my life's tapestry,
unravelling thread by thread.
As I wander the cruel corridors of fate,
feeling fragile, naked, alone,
I hold the hands of strangers
when I begin to lose my way, again and again,
on the long journey
home.

Atonement

When you were laid to rest,
I paused to contemplate
how much you had changed our world
with the way you lived and
words you would softly say.

Your advice, gently spoken, still rings true.
It gave us wise guidance to choose
to walk new paths,
to seek imagined goals,
to have strength to find our way.

Priceless treasures, memories,
yet I never took time to express
how much it all meant
when you dried our tears
and taught us how to pray.

So mother dear, I wish to atone
for feelings unspoken, contained.
Your heart should have brimmed
with equal doses of love
lavished on us
every day.

Audible World

The world is alive with sounds
that vibrate and swirl about,
like the soft patter of rain on glass,
making patterns as numerous as stars.

Listen to the wind
as it rustles through treetops
causing squirrels to scatter
as they chatter about.

There are some songs, soft as
snow falling or clouds
moving through the sky
that cool us down, refresh us.

Yet, some sounds wake us from our sleep,
like thunder symphonies,
filled with percussion, followed
by electric bursts of light.

The dogs begin to howl, en masse,
at the grand, ephemeral din
perceptible to those
with ears to hear.

Then the downpour follows,
big bangs on thin, tin roofs
and huddled people praying
for safety from the storm.

It passes and the pigeons come
to roost again,
cooing their joyful melody
when sun returns.

In homes, kitchen pots are banging,
cooking up a harmony of spicy delights,
and a baby's laughter echoes
through windows into the street.

In cities, many cars whiz by,
and taxis screech their horns.
Ladies heels clickity- clack,
people speak in many tongues.

Elevators beep a melody
as they reach each floor.
Cell phones with their multi-rings
Offer notes to the musical score.

Machines are purring and whirring,
an ambulance streams by,
playgrounds sing with high notes,
chirping birds assemble in choir.

The soothing sound that water makes
seems to calm the soul:
gurgling brooks, waterfalls,
in meditative repetition flow.

Our seas are a cacophony of sound
with intangible cadence all its own
from the high-pitched seagull chants
to the whales' deep mating calls.

But the daily sounds that we need to hear,
they flow, each a vital life source,
are the rhythmic beating of our hearts
and the ebb and flow of breath.

Celestial Journey

I thought that your constellation appeared
just before the moon took over the sky.
How did I miss knowing that your smile
could signal its early arrival
and allow the sunlight to warm the green hills
in suspended time?

Getting lost in that smile, and those special stars
you radiated as you walked,
it was magical, really,
the stuff that song lyrics hint at,
trying to immortalize an impossible feeling.

But you live in a multi-dimensional world,
never in one spot for long.
You've never pretended otherwise,
for you told me you are a seeker,
of wisdom that does not live here.

Your celestial journey is not mine.
I gain wisdom from earthly challenges,
through tests of courage, justice and
painful understanding of what it takes
to become lighter, truly human.

So here our sojourn ends,
for we have twin destinies,
and different paths to take
which ultimately will culminate
in that celestial place.

Children of Divorce

First, the fights begin,
high-pitched screams, loud banging,
voices too mumbled for me to hear
although I have my ear to the door,
wondering what caused the rage.
Was there danger lurking?
Could it be that my forgetting
to close the windows of dad's new car
after going out last night
and the wicked downpour that
gave it a premature cleaning
incited the torrent of emotion?
Or maybe I did something else,
something worse,
to pull them apart,
bring out their claws,
fill them with such hate.
If they separate,
what will happen to me,
to my sister,
sleeping in the room downstairs,
seemingly unaware
of the brutal altercation?
Careless words create
an irreversible rift,
making knife-like wounds
in their once-happy union
and deep in my heart.

Do they mean to kill each other,
kill our family dreams as well?
Don't they care for anyone anymore?
They finally said the word,
the one that leaves shame and blame
on the products of their nuptial tryst,
born of the stuff that once
made them laugh, admire each other,
make sweet love.
Now the scars must form
to protect us all from
drowning,
from losing our way
completely
in divorce.

Depression

Do not sink into darkness,
for I am here with you.
My heart is strong enough
to bring you back
to your point of sunlight.

I will bathe you in hope's radiance
by inviting your heart back to life,
one worth living.
In my arms, I feel you
shaking, breaking into tiny pieces.

After years of fighting the black of night
in solitude, take solace
in emptying your soul
of fears and fallacies.
Wash away the lies, see the truth.

You are a wonderful being,
rid yourself of any doubt.
Let others in to help you heal,
you can make your minutes count
by accepting the power of love.

Only you can choose a different path
and learn to savor life anew.
Your hug tells me you are longing
to believe, to accept, to know
the inner beauty
of you.

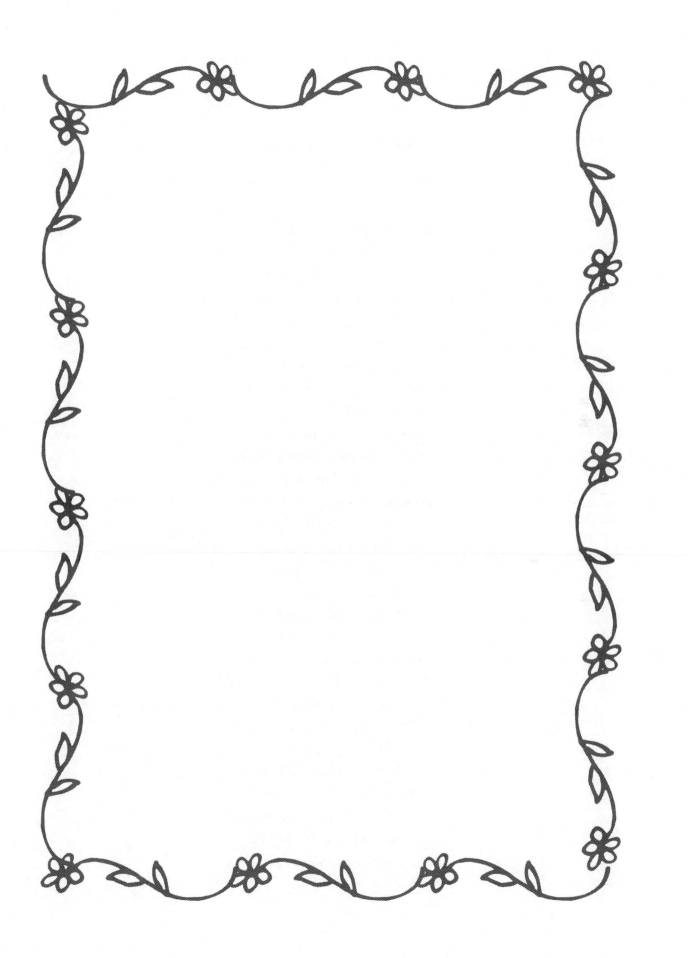

Emerald Dream

Climbing the hills of Inisfree
to a height reserved for angels and
the swallows that read our souls,
a rocky throne awaits.
As if in the confessional,
we pour out secrets of our sins and longings
to travel the great sea, to be a bird.
Gliding over perils below,
sharks with monstrous jaws
and demons desiring their fill,
we hold tight to our dreams of
exquisite bliss in our discoveries.
Below we pass ragged cliffs,
lands arid from the sun,
cries of famine, hate, and fear,
blood-stained opulence.
Then in our sights
a landscape appears
that beckons our approach.
Massive and diversified,
a tapestry of colors
moving toward an unseen goal.
Warm sweet air greets us there.
Our destination found.
But we are like gypsies,
penniless, wild,
to the folks who walk on by.
As we wander the markets
to quench our thirst for belonging,
prefering to barter, not beg,
I think of a way to get a day's pay.

Making music seems our best hope.
Tin whistle to our lips,
swaying our hips,
we play and whirl and glide.
A small child steps forward to share her bread
until mama pulls her aside.
I now know that we are not ready
to be strangers in a strange land.
Again we soar above the clouds,
above the world we roam
realizing that the bliss we seek
is the emerald treasure
called home.

Ethereal Dance

As evening folds into night,
twilight serves to connect
our dichotomous selves,
the dark and the light.

Cyclical changes
envelop the path ahead,
casting shadows
with unknown intent.

Now, nocturnal reflection must shine
wisdom to guide our steps,
balance our soul's twin yearnings
and enlighten our way
through silent, unconscious corridors
of the mind.

In cool, dark, spaces,
mental monsters lurk,
feeding on our private dreams,
sucking hope from our veins,
until the foe is vanquished.

Then our twin selves embrace
in the morning mist,
welcoming the promise
of another day.

Fantasy

As a breathless butterfly,
I will weave a castle in your arms
and enter a tower
directly to your heart.
We'll live blissfully together
drinking nature's nectar and
singing sweet love songs
that surge from deepest sea.
Neptune can bind us, man and wife,
as tides ebb and flow,
imitating life.
The waves, as they meet the shore,
enchant us with rhythmic melodies
of the conch, alluring and intoxicating.
Stormy seas, rocky shores, cannot sway
the moon from giving us
its lunar blessing,
for we are set apart,
as angels have been,
filled with grateful hearts
and endless praise.

Final Breath

If I must one day die
I wish that it be this way.
That you and I,
ripe in old age, rich in memories,
still sharing a love
that has taken many forms
over the years,
may clasp our winkled hands together
as if in prayer
and breathe our last breath
in unison.
And we shall hear
an angel's voice in song
guiding us to the Great Light,
My God.

Fledgling Poet

On the wings of imagination,
unspoken memories yearn to take flight,
beckoning you to unleash them,
pour them into your laptop all night.

Let hidden emotions empty
onto a Word doc, your new stage,
for you have become a dancer
spinning words onto the page.

Language allows your feelings
to find home in the ocean sea
or the starry skies, dazzling, white,
as you record them gracefully.

After resisting other writing tasks,
this outpouring seems cathartic, free
of judgment, words that can hinder
exposing your inner identity.

As an artist, you can reveal all your secrets
in dark purple, magenta, or cream,
they'll dazzle boldly or speak softly
of aspirations, hopes, and dreams.

Once you have opened the floodgates,
soul reflections as deep as a well
fill your poetry with music
of booming gongs and little bells.

As you taste more of life's salty tears
to mix with youth, so bittersweet,
as you deepen and grow, your work will also,
offering solace, necessary retreat.

So open wide your canvas, grab you brush,
new poet you are ready to embark
on a journey of linguistic pleasure
that frees you to leave your mark.

For when you open old wounds and fill up the cracks,
healing painful feelings begins
with the exhilaration of opening the heart
and letting the sunlight pour in.

Growing Wings

Run away, my son,
I sense your strong desire
to see the world, be wild.
So go
by boat, plane, by any means
into the seasonal changes
of places far beyond.
You will surely not rest
and the best of you must experience
freedom to grow.
And I will wait for your return,
for the knock upon my door
knowing that after a day,
you will have appetite for more
adventures far away
from this dwelling you call home,
a place of unconditional shelter
from the ugliest of storms.
Loaded in your backpack
is the steady devotion of those
whose love anchors you when needed
and rejoices silently
at your safe return.

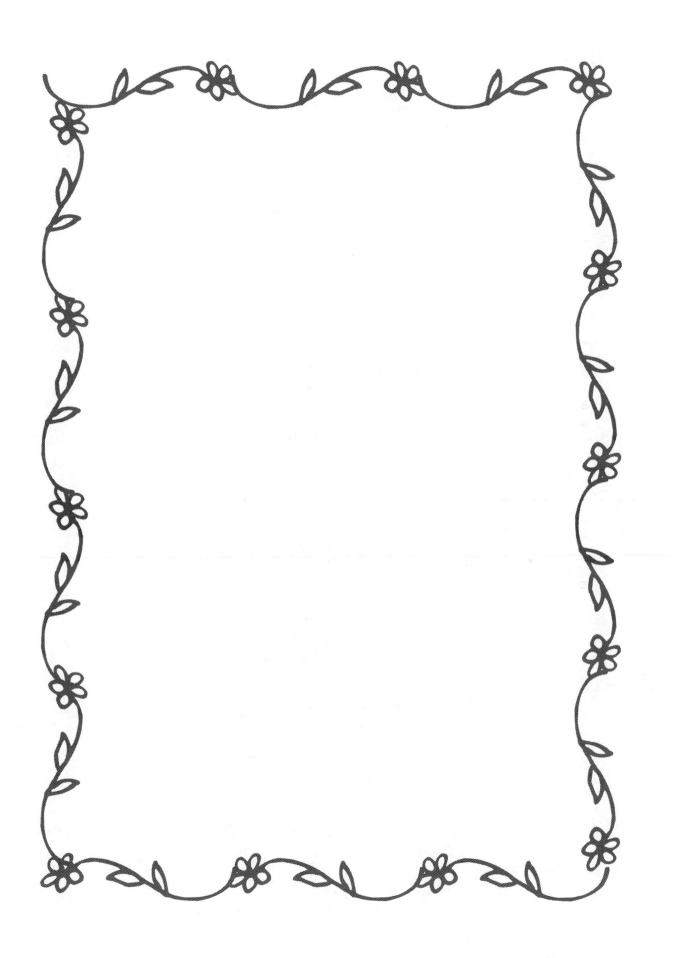

Higher Ground

Night falls, rivers flow,
and dark memories are released
like unchained ghosts
taking refuge in the stars.

The evening sky has wrapped us
in a diamond-studded blanket
while clouds shroud
the silent moon.

Stories are mapped
by constellations above,
astrological portrayals
of future possibilities.

But not for me,
for I am the shaper
of my destiny.
I never gave my power
to the darkness,
no matter its glitter and sparkle,
for I wish to find
a path with purpose
of my own.

One where truth lies
and lies can be discerned,
where hope lives
and breathes and beckons me
onward,
that I may continue
when I stumble,
become stronger through adversity,
navigate life's labyrinth,
and walk the walk
on higher ground.

Inner Armor

Staring
out a small window
onto the dusty road,
she waits for her life
to change,
for a chance to feel
anything
again.
It's been too long
since hope has lived
in her heart.
Regions of her body
are mapped with scars
and bluish-yellow bumps.
Love taps, he called them.
Yet the deepest scars are within,
holding her prisoner
of fear,
the kind that sucks out
any real hopes
of starting over.
She once had dreams
of a white knight,
true love,
of a marriage of body, mind, soul.
But her aching flesh
tells the naked truth
of these lies.
It screams of her need
to fit herself
with inner armor
and slay the monster,
and release his grip,
on her life.

Insomnia

As each evening settles in,
heralding time to rest,
my mind starts working overtime,
putting me to the test.

Lights are dimmed, soft music plays
a nocturnal melody,
but my adrenaline pumps,
my imaginations revs up,
and worries float unhampered, free

to haunt me in my chamber
as soft pillows surround my head,
wild thoughts scare away sweet slumber
pulling me out of bed.

I will read until my eyes tire,
maybe watch a tv show.
No, better yet, I'll meditate.
That surely will help me go

off to dreamland and desired rest.
Oops! I almost forgot
to finish the snack I'd meant to eat,
Then off to sleep I'll trot.

Of course, I should also finish up
the bills that need to be paid.
Then I can finally relax,
alertness is bound to fade.

I can crawl back into bed
feeling quite dead,
get rest before I must awake.
At my job, I'm not sharp,
my boss likes to carp
due to the toll insomnia takes.

To release its fierce grip
will take work on my part,
change my diet, get sleep therapy.
But no further can I slip,
I need strength of heart,
or ill and unemployed I will be.

Joshua Tree

High above,
vast earthy space
floats among the boulders,
San Jacinto Mountains,
and Joshua Trees.
In perfect balance,
these massive rocks, smooth and jagged,
have been placed by nature's hands.
Native American chants, ancient mysteries,
echo through crevices,
lyrics written in the desert sand.
Mid-day sun burns bright,
scorching tiny lizards as they hide
among the cacti,
all white flowering in April,
cooled by sudden winds.
Erosion-colored rocks, burnt orange, beige, grey,
and proud Joshua Trees, standing tall
against wild, flaring heat,
tell stories of a simpler time,
as nature serves to soothe the mind,
in reflective meditation
of the desert's quiet bliss.
Then night falls,
heralded by the howl of
coyotes and hawks,
beckoning
even the desert tortoise
to emerge from its sandy cave
to dance among the stone giants
sleeping silently under
starry sky.

Meaning of Why

When the body drifts
off to sleep and twilight
descends,
the heart is free to embrace
the self within
and float
on sturdy, invisible wings
into the land
where dreams
are born.
Divine music,
sweet and melodic,
drowns out chaos,
ego and lies,
about who you truly are,
child of eternity
born of celestial skies.
Absent is the greed,
the selfish pursuit
of whatever dispels the fear
of not finding satisfaction
but this fallacy becomes clear.

When survival of all
becomes as vital as one,
when we cease the need
to control
when we let our hearts flow
with compassion,
only then will we know
our true role
as peace seekers.
Life is not a problem
to solve,
but an ever-unfolding mystery
leading us to evolve
and taste, once again,
that delectable joy,
the essence of life,
the meaning of
why.

Millennials

All eyes are on you now, including your own,
as myriad selfies attest,
for you are the entitled generation
and you deserve the best.

You know rules are meant to be broken,
although solemn promises should not be.
When fleeting thoughts are keyed into cell phones
digital fingerprints can smear regrettably.

For the cloud feeds on Twitter, on Facebook
devouring text messages, twenty-four, seven.
The world is your playground through connections
that stretch from your laptop to heaven.

You're bright, energetic, ambitious,
excel in technology and tap,
play piano, soccer, and video games,
took art lessons, love hip-hop and rap.

Your global awareness is impressive.
Social justice issues, your concern.
Build homes for the poor, in US and Darfur.
From your example we all should learn

to make this world a better place,
create more jobs, increase the pay,
for the low wage earners and single moms,
while you rise to the top in a day.

With your college education,
your bravado, networking and more
you don't plan to start at the bottom.
You belong on the president's floor.

But patience is required as you step up.
Get experience, learn from the boss.
Let her discover how amazing you are.
Overconfidence can result in loss

of the self-esteem you've developed
from special grooming by well-meaning folks.
Step-by-step, you will fulfill your purpose
and give meaning to the millennial yoke.

Missing You

Bits of you are everywhere.
Your bed is strewn with favorite toys
and the blanket you dragged with you
as you maneuvered the house
still has your smell.
Blondish-red curls,
entwined here and there,
can still be found
in corners of rooms
we have yet to clean.
Your face looks longingly at us from photographs
framed in silver, precious as gold,
making us believe that any day now,
you will gracefully fly toward us,
as we receive your love,
open-armed and ecstatic,
once again.
We talk quietly of last Christmas,
how you got tinsel caught in your hair
and glistened playfully under the tree.
How you loved to outrun your buddies
and smell each backyard fragrance,
over and over.
But you are gone,
ravaged by disease that has caused
our hearts to bleed and cry
and want nothing more
than to have had one more hug,
another wet kiss,
before your last breath was stolen.

Your loss is most palpable
when we arrive home
and the big brass band,
the appreciative howls,
which heralded our arrival,
have been replaced
by sheer silence.
As you romp the Rainbow Heaven
made for dogs, loyal, loving, kind,
know that you have taken chunks of our hearts
now amply filled
with missing you.

Morning Muse

At five A.M., when the
sun has barely made its first appearance,
that's the time my inner muse
likes to awaken me to play.
Resentfully, I bury my face
in pillows, hoping to hide
but this invisible sprite is relentless

so wearily, I give in
and search my bedside drawer
for paper, pad and pen,
wishing for strong coffee,
and wondering what wisdom
can't wait for the alarm.

She whispers that
there aren't enough love songs.
Romantic longings are now seen as trite.
The young too need their fill
of idealistic hopes,
their share of magic that lasts.

Suddenly, the thought awakens
and dawns on me what I'm to do.
Students should celebrate sonnets,
amorous, lusty, moonlit poems
full of torment, mixed with kisses,
and endless hunger for lasting bliss.

Can Shakespeare, and Browning, and others
inspire youth to believe once again
in bonds too strong for betrayal?
Are they fearful of looking foolish
or do they simply fail to dream
of fulfilling love, yet unrequited?

I want the young to taste
from the cup of fidelity's joy,
sweet glue of twin shells that survive
rough waves, sandstorms, foragers,
holding onto each other with passion,
all the more beautiful whole.

Mountain Music

Starting slowly,
gliding easily,
breaking the silence with the soft "whoosh, whoosh",
as you sweep up sprays of glistening powder
at every turn.
Here and there, the sun catches snow crystals
turning them to diamond dust.
As you become one with the slope,
with its gradual descent,
it draws you into flowing, sensuous arcs
and makes you its lover.
Suddenly, magically, you feel the mountain's rhythm,
Hear the music deep within.
Flying and soaring,
laughing inside,
you have embraced the mountain's soul,
its rush, beauty, and majesty.
Fear has no potency now.
You are free to lose yourself
in the seduction
of skiing!

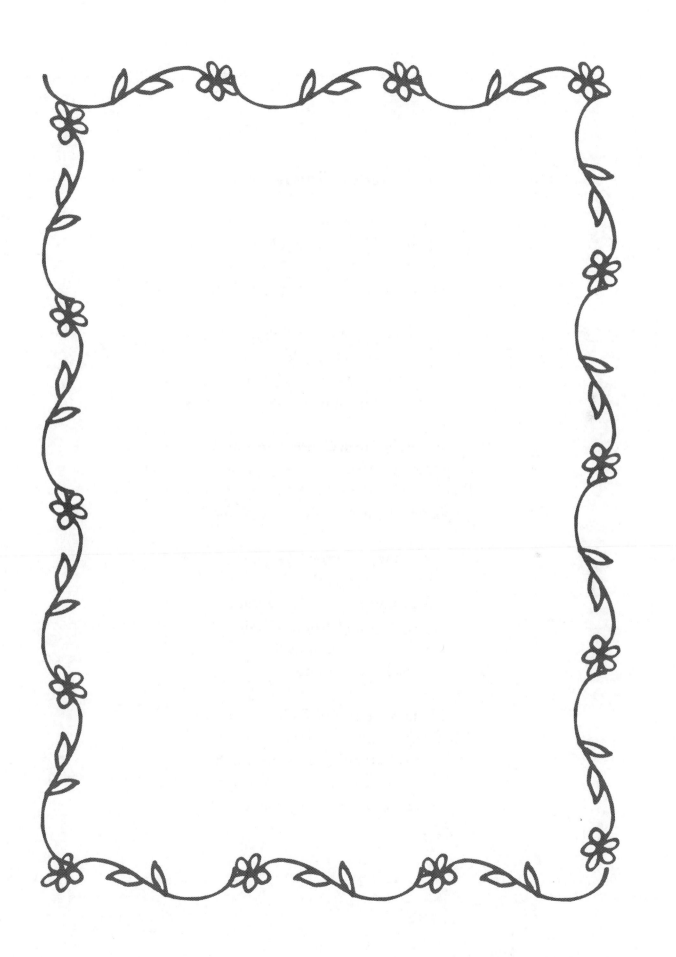

New Game

Sneaking up on me in the garden,
clinging to a gun in his fist,
my tiny son bursts into loud giggles
shooting mama with a cooling, fine mist.

For his fourth birthday,
he was given a purple popgun
to protect us from "bad guys"
who seem always on the run.

But at five, he had tested my limits
running around after wild game.
Toy rifle in hand, over went my plant stand,
shattered cruelly, only one to blame.

"I will kill you!" I said,
my face a bright red,
verbal venom I did not mean.
My toddling daughter's eyes
could not disguise
real fear of a murder scene.

"Mommy, don't do it!" she screamed,
aghast, swallowing fury and tears,
convinced that I had lost my mind.
How can such transformation occur
in a parent once loving and kind?

After regaining my grip,
reassuring my young
with hugs, kisses, apologies galore,
I saw how insidiously violence creeps
into our lives, speech, and society,
first with a giggle, then a roar.

So out went the potted plants
and weapons of destruction and shame
replaced by a "kiss gun" for pacifists
and a brand new family game.

This "gun", all sunny and blue,
was the gentle kind, as it should
shoot kisses at "bad guys", not bullets
always aimed at conversion to good.

Nicotine War

As you take a puff, get a nicotine rush,
the killing is silent and slow.
As it permeates each cell,
the tales it will tell,
of a one-sided battle.
Now hush!
Don't let the smoker get wise
to smokes clever disguise.
Advertisements cooly convey
relaxation is an aid,
forget the price to be paid,
while it feasts on every organ. Oh! Well.
But denial wears thin
when cancer starts to win,
and now it's a war of the poisons.
Nicotine began it all
and you took the fall.
Now you look to Chemo to end it.
Don't wait too long
before you write a life song
or a play with a better finale.
Escaping from its control is unthinkable
even from power so wrong.
But that's all in your head.
You can walk away.
Be strong, my love, be strong.

Night Terrors

There is a private island
where no man dare to go.
It exists in my mind's eye
and beckons me in slow
motion as I embark
and walk the sands of time
where ships have smashed and washed ashore,
yet none of them are mine.

What aspect of the angry seas
within my thoughts and tears,
disrupt my pleasant reverie
while sailors wait in fear?
Has Medussa been resurrected
to lure souls to disbelief,
killing trust, destroying bonds,
from which there's no relief?

From my private island,
I watch the tumultuous seas
feeling overwhelmed, shaken,
I fall upon my knees.
Oh! God, let dreams be reverent
filled with imagined bliss,
not mirror my darkest hours,
but display the lovers' kiss.

So I awaken to renounce
the night terrors hold on me,
basking in sun-splashed, cloudless sky,
my private island, now under the sea.

No Escape

The light through the window
casts shadows,
sinewy, silent,
exposing life outside,
amorphous, full of mystery.
Then nocturnal images return,
hidden thoughts, secrets to keep.
They haunt me as I make
my hasty retreat
down the same path
for the hundredth time,
catching my breath,
chasing the stars,
searching for
myself.

Offspring

Song of my soul,
my sweet longing
is for you to find
the road to your happiness.
Imprints of time passing
show in your lovely face
and yet I see
sadness in your smile.
So many features remind me
of my own youth;
The sparkle in your eyes,
your rosy cheeks,
almond eyes, pouting mouth.
Yet yours are put together
more gracefully, it seems.
Your teenage moods,
exhilarating and exhausting,
fill me with wonder.
Was I ever capable of so much
fire and ice?
Delighting in music,
fashion, fantasies,
new and fantastic,
you dance through life
to an alien beat.
I watch you rushing
full-spirited into the wind.
I sense the passion
in your soul,
in the dreams you weave,
and I admire your capacity for love.
You fill me with awe and gratitude
for being a precious part
of my world,
child of mine.

One Last Song

I know it isn't true
what they say about death,
that it creeps up behind you
and steals your last breath of life.
Not even death
could be so cruel, so heartless
as to give no warning
of his approach.
We all need time
to think things through,
and say goodbye
to those we love,
to sing
one last song.

Peace by Peace

Spirit,
your choice to be of earth
to manifest in flesh and blood
was bold
for your destiny,
now rooted deeply in the soil,
shaped in hard clay,
bears the scars of
wars, toil, strife,
as you strive to return
home
to the celestial light.

What will it take
for humanity to see
it's visage reflected in each other
instead of separate shards
from a shattered mirror?

We're prisms each
of various hues, shapes, sizes,
some smooth and benign,
others razor-sharp,
reflecting the full range
of humanity's potential,

each with immense potential
to ravage the planet,
destroy its own soul,
or join hands and hearts together
once again, peace by peace,
to become glorious,
whole.

Point of War

Casting shadows on killing fields
       flooded with blood and guts and shattered dreams,
Decaying men, once in their prime,
       send ghosts to console the mourners.
The bullet that ripped through his fine heart
       severed mine as well.
War's cold destruction cannot transcend
the widow's and the unborn's lament.
Cries from the womb at the sight of his tomb
bear witness to why it must end.
Have courage, they say,
   just look away, and remember
the point of it all.
Keep us all safe and free,
   what my love will never be,
      because he answered the call.

Private Lies

Lusting
for a sense of peace
not experienced for too long.
Impoverished, forgotten people
at war with a world
clouded by hate,
tearing lives asunder.
Muslim, Christian, Jew,
the list goes on.
War's insatiable atrocities,
fueled by misunderstanding,
hunger for power,
love of greed.
But too often at home
in our intimate lives,
we close our doors
and our hearts.
Dissecting each other
with cruel words,
silent coldness,
we are no better there.
The killing is gradual,
insidious,
still wearing the pretense of love.
Our private lives
once so admired by all,
begin to crack
and reveal
our private
lies.

Questions of Desperation

What strange saturation of light
illuminates the visions
of communal strife
painted on city murals
for all to see?
Is it moon or street lamp,
sunbeams or shadows,
that best reveal urban plight?
Sordid odors, ashes of the dead
faces of people crying out
in dark corners,
penniless, forgotten,
with their whole estate packed
in a plastic bag.
What is the worth of a soul
mad with rage, hunger, grief,
unemployed, unemployable,
crazy from sad fate?
How can we ease their
desperation?

Remember

Remember that balmy evening last spring,
the one we thought would never come,
when we walked home
from a movie in town
and we talked for miles?
I asked you how you found my number
after so many years.
You smiled, and I knew
you must have kept it
in your left shirt pocket,
closest to your heart,
waiting for the courage to call.

We laughed about childhood pranks,
silly jokes we played, never meaning harm,
you made sure of that.
Somehow I sensed that your heart
had grown even bigger,
big enough to encompass us both.
But then you told me
the hard truth that you had buried
deep within.
Suddenly, my mind went numb,
I could not hear your words,
only feel the catharsis of your sobs,
pouring out buckets of pain
about your cancer battles
onto the street,
making a river.

It swept us up and carried us along,
speechless for a while,
and then I fell into your chest
and through your soul.

There, I felt at home,
as you encircled me, us both,
with little stars
and whispered that death
is but a door
to our greater selves
and promised that our love
would see us through.

Roses and Babies Breath

The unraveling of her mind
was inevitable
once she had learned
that you had become part
of the sky.
You were her apple blossom,
her whole rose garden,
her reason to always find home
even when tired or lost or far away.
But you've vanished
riding the wind, swept out to sea.
An image of your smile is
all that remains
to warm the wilted flowers.
How can a just God allow
a baby's breath to cease?
Couldn't some divine force
have held your head up
so creeping SIDS could not
steal your last gasp,
eroding all joy,

creating immeasurable pain.
With steel knife, it has ripped out
her heart,
piece-by-piece,
this cold, relentless blade
of infant death.

Seekers

We are searchers,
silent music makers
followers of dreams.
Often, we are unaware
of the power of the human spirit,
the sweet miracles to come.
It is not necessary to understand
how the heart is able to mend
when shattered by love's deception
or ravaged by rage or fear.
Somehow spring finds its way
out of the darkness
into life's saving grace,
hope renewed
once more.

Separate Shores

Consumed by deep desire,
tempered by limits of time and space,
I revel in the euphoric memories
of our entwined embrace.
Nothing else mattered.
As I sit on the beach
watching tides ebb and flow,
I curse their ill-timed patterns.
Their moon-lit tables have ignored
the rhythms of my heart.
My yearnings, naked, exposed,
to the winds, raw cold,
are now buried in the sand.
But passion knows no limits.
Only the soul can perceive our mind,
contain the heart,
so we can trust ourselves
and others.
Like the phoenix rising from the ashes,
these feelings well up
and pool in bittersweet tears
of love's loss.
Yet I realize
it cannot be that simple, sanitized, clean.
Choking back salty tears of futility,
I declare:
I respect distance,
understand obligation and dual desire,
believe in destiny,
and sadly, accept our reality.
So we are bound
to separate lives,
left to dream of an extraordinary love
and cherish a memory
of incomplete joy.

Sighs and Whispers

In whispered sighs,
your love poured into me
like gentle rain that transforms
into burning desire.
So safe, so pure a connection,
of bodies and souls.
Sweet satisfaction,
mutual, harmonious rhythms,
hips swaying to inaudible music
of earthly bliss.
What magic draws me to you
as my heart takes flight?
It dances tenderly, gracefully,
over the hills and valleys
of our bodies,
moving as one.
Ignite the passions of my heart,
quench the fire in my bones.
Hold me close enough to fill me
with your power, your hunger,
insatiable lust.

My intimate touches trace
the outline of your face,
parting those sensuous lips,
still trembling, wet,
and desiring to be
swallowed up
in your smile.

Silent Farewell

The first day he was gone,
I barely noticed,
but as time sped by,
I ached in the space left behind,
like a hole cut out of the sky.
Suddenly, breathlessly, I missed him
without knowing why.

I grew afraid of premonitions,
of some evil lurking about
ready to suck all goodness
from the air in our lungs
ballooning in and out.

I called his name, gave a silent scream
that only his heart could discern
but no response came forth
so I began to dream

that he was a young child,
lost among carnival booths,
speeding rides, whirligigs,
flashes that blind to the truth.

So I must pray that all is right,
bid farewell to my anguished fright.
Forge ahead, no need to fret,
cling to sweet memories, never forget.

Sleeping with a Stranger

I swore that I would never
end up in bed with a man
unknown and unknowing
but somehow it happened.

Staring at his rugged face,
sleep-filled eyes,
deep lines in his face,
I see the map of a life rich in experience,
a being, disturbing and new,
with lips parted in nocturnal bliss
as if ready to reveal his identity,
and secrets of his soul.

Now, out of deep regret,
fear or rational response,
should I quietly leave this chamber
and run before he wakes?

Run from ancient struggles
of family ties that bind.
Am I strong enough to suppress
this self-centered flight?

Or should I embrace these changes
in the man I now recognize
as different yet familiar
from decades of change
that have shaped us anew.
My life partner,
my spouse.

Standing Tall

Would you still love me
if you knew I was dying
to old beliefs,
long-cherished values,
rich in childhood history?

Could you possibly understand
that ideas we shared when young
are no longer credible to me
despite my strong conviction
years ago?

Since leaving home, I have shed
layer by layer,
the cozy cocoon
mother wove 'round us,
for love is blind.

My new eyes see differently
and butterfly wings have freed me
to explore in more depth,
over many miles,
what my journey must be.
Suddenly it became clear
that comforts of mediocrity,
the beauty of
manicured lawns,
did not suit me.

Now I clearly see the self-interests
that keep us from standing tall,
the kind that provide insulation
from feeling the pain
of injustice at the heart
of it all.

So when I am far away
mending the bones and hearts
of destitute people
riddled with deception and disease,
will you reconcile yourself
with the ugliness, with truth?

People, a world away
lose much that they hold dear,
family members, community, lovers,
and in sheer desperation,
all faith in mankind.

Fault me, if you must,
for yearning
to be emptied, used up,
to help those whose hope
in the future
died long ago.

Injustice cannot endure
once enough people
hear the cries
that reverberate
and affect us all.

Stillness Speaks

The quiet space,
the one you choose,
on mountaintop or in a crowd,
a place where stillness speaks
in silent tongue, angelic song,
precious in its ability
to remove the mental clutter,
obstacles to growth,
to finding inner happiness,
to creation of positive thought.

For intention of the mind
is potent.
It can shape humanity's future,
calm the raging beast,
spread faith that had been lost,
or incite a tempest
of malevolence
which has a bloody cost.

Each heartbeat can bring us closer,
to our common silence,
saving breath.
For we all share
the same air
and gaze at the same sky.

If we allow stillness in,
we all might win
common wisdom,
serenity,
joy.

Stiletto

The sound of shattered glass
fills the empty space
between screams and ugly promises.
I'm told to just turn a few tricks.
Don't think, don't feel.
Get enough cash, make the deal.
Will you buy me red stilettos
and a stuffed brown teddy bear,
to cuddle at night
when no one and nothing else cares?
Since I ran from home,
from abuse, tears, and drugs,
I've found new sources of pain.
Pimped and pounded all night
for attempting flight.
Submission and control do reign.
Life laced with fears
I return to the streets,
close my eyes and pretend
I'm not there.

Broken, stoned, no way out,
no reason to try
to get clean.
Should I give up hope
to find a good home
before I turn
fourteen?

Strawberry Love

Hello! Strawberry love
I miss your kiss,
your soft, sweet, savory smile.
It melts upon my lips
and burns there 'til we meet again.
Although I count the days
that feel like years,
I want you to know
that I wish you good spaces
in the faraway places you go.
No distance, no lapse of time,
will ever erase
the deliciousness
of your ice creamy love.
Double scoop,
please.

Student Voices

Hey ! teach
You want to learn
who I am,
why I'm here
where I'm heading
are my goals clear?

Well, to be honest
(whisper, don't shout)
I'm still trying
to figure that out.

Excitement
mixed with fear,
these first steps are rough,
I'm capable, I'm willing,
but the work load is tough.

Obese textbooks, stuffed with ideas
I'll never learn them all!
No more fast-food diet
of spoon-fed special ed.
It's now to cram or fall.

Textbooks are wet
with my own sweat
and the tears of too much to learn.
Help me relate
to the texts I hate
or my mind will crash and burn!

These small desks feel like prisons to me.
Free my spirit, feed my soul.
Help me to write my own life script
or I'll never reach my goal.

My pencil is sharpened,
I'm ready to fly.
Send my imagination soaring.

I want to thrive,
keep my dreams alive.
Please don't say anything boring!

Sliding along icy ground,
leaping gaps in my knowledge,
trying to catch up, get my footing,
make it right in college.

Ma has always had faith in me,
Dad says "Work hard, be strong".
Friends tell me to follow my dream,
time to write my own song.

Sometimes the lyrics of music I love
tell my story, the joy and the pain
of working two jobs, a kid to support,
I must master this game.

My heroes, my supports,
they believe I can succeed,
yet it all comes down to asking
"Where will it all lead?"

A good career is what I want,
satisfaction, help others, good pay.
Want to take control of my life
find happiness in my own way.

Help me aim high
for the stars, the sky,
squelch all lingering doubts.
Overcome this frustration,
get to graduation.
That's what this journey's about.

A Sustainable Life

Tread softly
lest anyone hear
you brush past the bush,
your turn of the latch.

Climb up to my window
open, willing to release
me to new callings,
more exhilarating,
resplendent with uncertainty,
ripe with hope.
Untethered, fly me on endless wing
above vast unchartered lands,
serene seas, verdant valleys,
and mountains adorned with snow.

You can take me away,
I'm ready to go
but do not fail to hold me
until my wings can support
half the world
impoverished, victimized, dead
to any hope of
sweet survival.

For I know that from birth, some have no escape
from humanity's brutal blows
and from nature's cruel fate,
add famine and floods to the hate,
with power to break bones and men's will.

Magicians called teachers can transform
what was arid into arable gold.
Build a well, find the streams
that run deep within.

For only honest, clean water can quench
the desperate thirst of the innocent
and with renewed opportunity for the poor,
wash away humanity's sins.

Now my journey has truly commenced.
I have ridden the wind, harnessed the sun,
committed to aiding the cause
of fairness, care, and strife
to support fellow humans, wherever they're born,
to have a sustainable life.

The Alchemist

Caught in your gaze
I am drawn into the cerulean depths
of continents, magical orbits
staring in starry wonder.
What treasures do you seek,
what intangible dreams do you weave,
as you follow the moon by night?
Are you listening to your heart
as you swim against the tides,
sinking through tears and years
of broken promises?
Do not drown in your sorrow
for you possess inner light,
enough to guide you
to safety, back to joy.
Hold fast to the horizon
as you walk on solid ground.
Be nourished by the wisdom
of your soul, the alchemist
who can transform and heal
and refill the emptiness.

Thirst for Spring

Welcome! Heralds of spring
after the long frost,
grey days, too many to count,
giving way to turquoise delights.
The red-breasted robin's song,
nascent buds
bursting through tips
of sweet magnolia branches,
crocus clusters
peeking up from wet soil
after heavy rains
and rainbows that follow
showing off ribbons of vibrant colors.
These images become parts of us,
our outlook improving, as the
green meadow sprinkles with buttercups
giving hearts refreshment.
The wildflowers begin to bloom
oranges, reds, purple and gold
like the sunlit dome, sending
sun showers to quench
our deep thirst
for spring.

Twisted Fate

Mama, can you hear me?
I want to understand
why I am destined to be in your womb
soon to inhabit this barren land.
Fetching water each day from miles away
you carry jugs in a somber mood,
plodding on raw, blistered feet,
starving for a morsel of food.
With malaria, TB, so rampant,
death is no stranger here.
What sliver of hope keeps you going?
Underneath I sense your great fear
that greed has blinded the affluent world
which consumes more than it needs,
ignoring the cries of impoverished souls,
undernourished, ripe for disease.
So when I am released from this womb,
and suckle your empty breast,
am I likely to end up in an early tomb?
Why endure this painful quest?

Wanderlust

My wanderings seek no end,
I'm mesmerized by a strange light,
so I follow persuasive longings,
I become like a bird in flight

over earth's vast spaces, sacred traces,
while hearing an ancient muse,
I'm lured to follow sublime reverie
that cannot be refused.

Damp moss, arid soil, caress my toes,
also rocks, warm sand, and loam.
My fingers outline the beauty of sky,
the all enclosing, azure dome.

My head's in the clouds,
the heart hungers for more
exquisite sensations,
memories stored,
undulating cadence
of new foreign chants,
most magical of syllables
on my lips will dance,

along with succulent flavors
frolicking on my tongue,
each a culinary temptress
for which operas are sung.

Sumptuous meals, exotic dance,
landscapes that stretch to the sea,
majestic mountains, valleys deep,
I cannot contain my glee.

As I feast my eyes, my senses are primed
to recall every minute, each day.
Turning to night, sleepy sunlight
brings me to journey's end.

Watchful Creator

As we indulge in blissful meanderings
through shaded trail or meadows
capricious flowers stand in attention,
listening to the songs of bluebirds
that sweetens the June air.
All seems right with the world.

What eyes seem to follow our every move,
careful to observe
our reverence for fragile nature?
So humble, yet spectacular to imbibe
like the color of water, or rich magenta skies
intoxicating our wanderings
fueling tactile desires.

So much of what nature teaches
is imperceptible, it seems
yet we fill our senses to the brim,
take a tantalizing swim,
as audacious consumers of God's holy work
until our voracity is satisfied.

Ways of Knowing

How can we teach
our children to dance
when we have not practiced the steps
or recall the pure bliss
of a lover's first kiss
as we swept each other
'round the dance floor?

How can we inspire
our children to sing
in melodic, hypnotic ways
that capture one's imagination,
visualizing notes in a starry daze?

How can we watch
our chidren grow
and not fill their minds
with hunger for expression
that only in art they will find?

The exhilaration of the sunrise,
in music, painting or poem,
may help them to cope,
provide hearts with hope
when lost or far from home.

Let's dance and sing
and create artfully
so our children can discern
from our actions more than lectures,
heart rhythms from which to learn.

What If

What if I had not accepted your hand
after meeting your starry glance,
and our lives had never entwined
as we chose to enjoy the dance?

What if I had run away,
taken the nearest plane
to live as a dazzling artist
alone in the south of Spain?

Creating, like Gaudi, new visions,
new ways of seeing the world,
instead of deciding to settle down,
my wings could have unfurled.

But since things are very often
not simply black or white,
what if we could see both aspects,
sunlit day and darkest night?

Looking back and pondering
what might have been and why
inflames the imagination
but is futile as the sky

when clouds float by illusively,
hiding its true color, blue.
So make the most of who you've become,
not wish to be someone new.

Winds of Change

Winter frost gives way to spring
just as we were about to lose hope
of the robins return.
Sunlight beckons us forth
out of dreary grey into greens and gold.
The skies are filled with birds now,
and the melodious discussions
of wrens, chickadees, sparrows,
coloring the treetops
now bursting with tiny leaves.
The world is alive again!
Myriad songs of nature's rebirth
splashed with warmth,
cooled with showers,
can be heard in the distance,
melting the self-centered ways
of the shut-ins
who stuff their bellies and minds
with winter clutter
trying unsuccessfully to avoid
the winds of change.

Word Art

Write poetry as lyrics,
words blending into song,
melodies of floating notes,
harmonious compositions,
how living sounds.

Paint poetry as artists do
with pen as painter's brush.
Splashes of colorful phrases,
images, dark, sensuous, wild,
vivid memories, future dreams.

Sculpt your stories carefully
each line, precious detail
to express life's deepest emotions,
passions, screams, and
the magical wonders.

Dance to the hip-hop of word play,
feel free, fly all over the floor,
pulsating beats of each stanza
life moving on,
steps in time to each score.
Create a blanket of interwoven threads,
dark days lightened with joys,
a holistic piece that illuminates
your inner radiance and speaks
from your soul.

Your Smiling Face

I search your face, look into your eyes,
to find vestiges of the smile
that could always hold me in its spell.
It gladdened my being,
as those pouting lips erupted
into the grin I know so well.

I wonder where the years have gone.
They slipped by without a warning,
inaudible steps cover the map of our lives,
while new paths for you were forming.

Staring at found photographs,
I hold proof and savor those hours
of your precious innocence,
as you ran through the wildflowers.

So now you're all grown up, it seems
and your life journey has commenced.
You're ready to live out adult dreams.
with intelligence, good sense.

Your wings of independence
were long-coming, and hard earned.
I'm proud to have been a steady source
of some of what you've learned.

As you depart, leave the memories
that allow me to retrace
your delicate steps in time
so I may enjoy repose
in your smiling face.

About the Author

Mary R. Callahan is presently teaching Language and Literature classes at Bucks County Community College in Newtown, Pennsylvania. For most of her career, she has worked with students who have struggled to master reading, written expression, and general language skills due to a variety of learning disabilities. After studying English as her major in college, Mary attended Teachers College, Columbia University, in New York City where she received her Master's degree in Special Education. She recently completed a doctoral degree in Special Education at Arcadia University (PA.). Her passion is to enhance the communication skills of students of all ages and particularly, to inspire a deep appreciation of the joy and power of effective reading and writing in individuals with educational difficulties. For her, poetry has been a delightful unfolding of feelings, observations, reactions to world events, and ideas sparked by literature. She believes that there is a hidden poet in everyone.

As Raold Dahl has stated (in The Minpins):

Above all, watch with glittering eyes the whole world around you because the greatest secrets are always hidden in the most unlikely places. Those who don't believe in magic will never find it.